Becoming A Conscious Business Game Changer

A Mini Handbook Guide of Simple Concepts For Strategically Changing The Rules in Next Level Business Frameworks

Alicia "WATERS"

Copyright © 2014 Alicia "WATERS"

All rights reserved. Except for use in the case of brief quotations embodied in critical articles and reviews, the reproduction or utilization of this work in whole or part in any form by any electronic, digital, mechanical or other means, now known or hereafter invented, including xerography, photocopying, scanning, recording, or any information storage or retrieval system, is forbidden without prior written permission of the author and publisher.

The scanning, uploading, and distribution of this book via the Internet or via any other means without permission of the publisher and author is illegal and punishable by law. Purchase only authorized versions of this book and do not participate in or encourage electronic piracy of copyrighted materials. Your support of the author's rights is appreciated.

Names, characters, places, and incidents are based on the author's own personal experience therefore names of persons and entities remain unnamed to protect the integrity of the story and the privacy of those involved. Any group or organization listed is for informational purposes only and does not imply endorsement or support of their activities or organization.
For ordering, booking, permission, or questions, contact the author.

www.anwempires@gmail.com
www.amazon.com/author/alicianwaters

ISBN:13:978-1495413223

Printed in the United States of America by Create Space

Becoming A Conscious Business Game Changer

Dedication & Acknowledgment

This book is a general dedication to all of the conscious business game changers who are on the journey of achieving their highest levels of success in their entrepreneurial endeavors.

I give thanks and acknowledgments to God and all who have enriched my entrepreneurial adventure.

Table of Contents

Introduction: The Ultimate Sacrifice of Being a Conscious Entrepreneur

Patience Persistence & Perspiration Create More Consciousness in Business

Are You a Conscious Business Game Changer?

Your Sky Is Your Limit for Your Business Expansion

Are You Asleep in Your Business Agenda?

Awaken to Your Lower Hanging Fruit in Your Business

Conscious Intentional Business Blogging Increases Your Impact & Income

Never Be Afraid to Change the Rules in Your Business Agenda

Try A Nonlinear Approach to Marketing

Learning How to Color Outside the Lines

Conclusion: Changing the Rules

Introduction

The Ultimate Sacrifice of Being A Conscious Entrepreneur

The ultimate sacrifice of being a conscious entrepreneur is being willing to live a few years of your life like most people won't so that you can spend the rest of your life living like most people can't.

Like many others, in my early years of becoming a conscious entrepreneur, there were a lot of sacrifices of time, money and shame around not making money. Sometimes not having the resources to launch myself into bigger arenas caused me to feel inadequate. Yet the greatest results were produced in my personal and professional transformation.

The journey of personal and professional mastery taught me the patience of waiting on something far greater than I was originally planning for in my business. The ultimate sacrifices are now creating my heaven on earth in my personal and professional life.

Today, I have a multipurpose business that serves diverse industries and is now on record to be a seven-figure business within the first six months of its re-launch. So, the years of sacrifices of going without, re-working my business frameworks and re-launching a bigger empire was well worth it.

The patience of living a few years off the traditional grid has now landed me and so many other conscious entrepreneurs into the lifestyles that we played a part in co-creating. Yet greater than we could have ever imagined.

Becoming A Conscious Business Game Changer

Patience Persistence & Perspiration
Create More Consciousness in Business

The late and great Napoleon Hill was one of the most consciously aligned entrepreneurs of all times. His famous quote, "Patience, persistence, and perspiration makes an unbeatable combination for success." This will continue to be a timeless wisdom enhancer for all eras of entrepreneurs.

I believe that patience, persistence, and perspiration also help to create more consciousness in your business, through discipline, greater awareness along with developing your mental muscles of determination.

When I apply the "Triple P" Factor, especially as it relates to the area of patience, something much more expansive always unfolds and provides me with an invitation to be more awake and conscious of higher quality opportunities that I would have missed if I would have executed hastily or out of alignment.

Though no one is probably a huge fan of waiting, I've learned over the years that when it comes to having a flourishing/thriving business, patience is the fuel that allows persistence and perspiration to complete its course of excellence.

Often, Spirit would tell me to have some patience because trying to force life to unfold faster than it is meant to be is futile. I've had to call forth patience often and let it move at its own pace for the unfolding of my personal and professional affairs. So, call forth your "Triple P" Factor to achieve your overall success.

Your Sky Is Your Limit
For Your Business Expansion

There is an old saying that the sky is the limit. I created a coaching program several years ago, that I've now turned into a new consulting practice and a book entitled, Your Sky Is Your Limit. That concept is truer than ever when it comes to business expansion.

Though there is an open sky of unlimited possibilities for everyone, it is all about your own personal sky of having an expanded consciousness in order to co-create the business and lifestyle that you desire.

Every single day is a conscious business game changer day to tap into our inner genius to go beyond our limits and push ourselves beyond the edge of our comfort zones to launch ourselves into realms of success that are only unimaginable.

Again, this is about your sky of unlimited possibilities and not what is available for others. Your unique path for business is designed for you to be limitless in your own authenticity to succeed.

Call to Action:

Create greater expansion this week in your business by applying more consciousness to your planning as you move forward.

Are You a Conscious Business Game Changer?

Are you a conscious business game changer? I've had to ask myself several times that very question as I'm stepping up more into my pioneer essence. Like most, I've tried several business strategies that did not work.

I don't believe that there is any one size fits all framework for your business agenda. Though many of the traditional business formulas have worked in the past, some are irrelevant for the current or next era of business success.

There comes a time when you have to change the rules to begin pioneering a higher/advanced way of getting things done with greater awareness. Being totally conscious of your business agenda and not being afraid to change the rules of as a pioneer entrepreneur is what is going to separate you from the non-conscious corporate pack or cookie cut frameworks out there.

So, are you a conscious business game changer?

How do you know if you're one or if it's your time to become one?

5 Insights to know that you are a conscious business game changer or ready to become one:

1. None of the current business models have worked for you after putting them into practice over time. You feel that almost everything that you see in the current business models needs to be up-leveled and you're trying figure out how you can create a new way.

2. When you feel guided to bring your awakened spiritual practices into your business agenda from a non-religious perspective, but rather as a foundational integration for infusing Source power for holistic success.

3. You use non-traditional tools and models that seem to have nothing to do with your business but actually help your business become successful.

4. You stay in hyper creativity mode (with a few frustrations for trying to figure things out). You know that there is a better/more relevant way to generate a successful business and lifestyle, but you haven't quite figured it all out.

5. You're up late most nights and/or trying to figure out all during the day how you're going to be successfully set apart in business after you've tried everything you know possible.

So, the question remains; Are you a conscious business game changer or becoming one?

Are You Asleep in Your Business Agenda?

Are you asleep in your business agenda? If so then wake up already. Though most conscious entrepreneurs are usually awakened by certain aspects of their personal lives or daily routines, they are often still very much asleep in their business agendas.

When is the last time you've had a major wake up call to occur that showed you where you were asleep to several opportunities? Opportunities that could have allowed you to make a bigger impact on those you serve or would have increased your income massively, but you missed them.

If you're in business and you haven't had that happen yet, trust me you will experience a few wake-up calls and especially if you aren't awake in your business agenda.

3 Ways to Avoid a Harsh Wake Up Call

1. Keep a conscious business journal. This is a journal that is used strictly for your business brainstorming, emotional release around your business agenda and also recording insights from spiritual guidance or intuition about next steps.

2. Create a conscious monthly business plan based on your explorations and discoveries from your journaling. Make sure that your business plan has a now and later framework that keeps you focused on creating your now wealth and impact while working on your bigger business endeavors that take more time.

3. Enroll a conscious business mentor for accountability along with building a conscious team to create continuous awakened energy within the business.

Becoming A Conscious Business Game Changer

Call to Action:

Spend some time over the next few weeks bringing more awakened energy to your business through journaling and creating a conscious business plan. Use your intuition to infuse your business in a more profound way.

Awaken to Your Lower Hanging Fruit
In Your Business

Are you awaken to your lower hanging fruit in your business? Often, business owners are always focusing on the bottom line and the end of the days' big results. This type of focus is perfectly fine as long as it's balanced with the awareness of other present moment possibilities.

Though there is a lot of money to be made in your current brilliant business ideas, don't ever despise the lower hanging fruit that was actually present long before the bigger picture of your wealth increase unfolded. This lower hanging revenue, for example, is like a non-signature product or service. This is the money that is part of your "Now Harvest," yet, most business owners overlook their lower hanging fruit because they've been full bloom driven.

They're too busy looking up and not looking down or with a holistic panoramic view to see what lower hanging fruit could be the seeds for a bigger investment in your business. Because most business owners are asleep in their agendas, by the time they wake up to realize that the lower hanging fruit was there all of the time, like regular fruit, over time it has withered away. They come to realize that they either ignored or took their first profits and did not use them wisely. In doing so they allowed the proceeds to dwindle.

Wake Up Call to Action:

This week look at your business agenda with more consciousness to see if there is some lower hanging fruit/money for you to reap in the present to help launch you from where you currently are in your business to where you want to be.

Becoming A Conscious Business Game Changer

Conscious Intentional Business Blogging Increases Your Impact & Income

Blogging is one of the fastest growing and lucrative industries for writers of all kinds to get their messages out to the world. Blogging is very important and the writing process provides a greater sense of awareness for evolution than most people know.

I am an avid blogger and at times blogging has really and truly been my saving grace when I don't know which direction I should take when it comes to reaching my goals. Every time I find myself getting very concerned about my forward movement, a small voice always says, just write, just blog.

Yet, there comes a time where you must align your blogging with pure intentionality as it relates to your business endeavors with a higher level of consciousness. Blogging for business is not just about blogging to try to gain more clients or make a sale with one of your amazing products, it also about creating a conscious community with others who share similar expertise. It's great to align or join forces with others and possibly see how you both can work together to empower more people and make it lucrative for both parties as you add value to the world.

I believe in also creating what I call conscious business transparency as it relates to blogging for income, opportunities or connections. Don't ever sell yourself short just to add value. Everyone has to make a living and deserves to achieve their highest levels of success. Again, being intentional in your energy displays your integrity and the people whom you attract will know it and respect it because they also desire to be valued.

Becoming A Conscious Business Game Changer

Your target audience will follow you and pay for your services. The more you increase your impact on their lives the more they will help to increase your income. Being intentional with them in your content will show them just how focused you are on their total well-being.

Call to Action:

Consider bringing more consciousness and intentionality to your blogging for business. Spend some time connecting with your intuition to co-create the process that is going to be unique for your business blogging endeavors.

Never Be Afraid to Change the Rules In Your Business Agenda

The world of business is constantly changing as fast as technology does. This is why conscious business game changers stay ahead of the game with a great awareness of this rapid continuum. They realize that the rules are always meant to be altered or advanced.

Some business owners are afraid to change the rules in their current business agenda because they aren't sure what the payoff will be from the risks that are taken. Fear often grips many because they've tried so many strategies in the past that didn't pay off.

Now, most operate from paralysis and won't take their past failures as a universal invitation to awaken them to the inner pioneer that is telling them to not only change the rules but create new rules of engagement for others to model after in their own authenticity.

Never allow the fear of not knowing what to do stop you from showing up in your business as a change agent who is ready to serve, provide value to others and lead the way as a successful business owner.

Call to Action:

The number one step to begin changing the rules is to change your *"Mindset"* about what is possible in the present, as well as the future. Increase your awareness of the limiting beliefs that you might have.

Becoming A Conscious Business Game Changer

Expand your mindset through listening to audios or reading materials that will assist you with seeing your business and yourself from a holistic success vantage point.

Or better yet, create the resources from your inner wisdom to provide you with the answers that you can turn around and share with others.

Spend some time over the next few weeks thinking of ways that you can change the rules to your advantage along with developing a consistent practice for mindset and business expansion.

Try A Nonlinear Approach to Marketing

When it comes to the subject of marketing, I've found over the years that it's not about always following a simple step by step formula or linear format to bring the results that you desire.

Sometimes you have to try a nonlinear approach and use your marketing efforts in a completely different way. In Luke 19:30 New King James Version (NKJV) it says; "Go into the village opposite you, where as you enter you will find a colt tied, on which no one has ever sat. Loose it and bring it here.

Sometimes you have to go and market in an arena that you've never considered. It's called crossover-marketing or sub-niche marketing. This is where you expand outside of your normal target audience to add value in new territories, gain more exposure and do something different than what is being done by other so-called experts.

Call to Action:

Take some time to connect intuitively with your inner money wisdom to discover or explore nonlinear ways to market more effectively.

Learning How to Color Outside the Lines

Sometimes in business, we take things too serious, desiring to be in control of the details and every aspect of trying to accomplish our dreams. We look for linear processes to provide us with every step on how to get from where we are to where we desire to be. However, sometimes we have to become a house off the grid to get re-aligned for a greater unfolding.

Life desires to gives us our highest and best good at all times even when the contrast present seems to be displaying the opposite of our highest levels of fulfillment. Often, our business is calling us upward to live and serve from a much more upgraded and expanded expression which can be a very non-traditional process for achieving.

Sometimes we have to interrupt ourselves and began to take an outside of the box approach to achieve our holistic success. If you've ever observed young children coloring, they will tend to color outside of the lines and it's perfectly fine with them. I believe entrepreneurs can learn a lot from having a childlike essence. We need to relax and learn not to take things so seriously. We need to begin coloring outside of the lines to come up with more creative ways to allow our next levels of business success to unfold effortlessly into our highest desires.

We don't always have to have everything perfect or conform to the illusion of looking like we have everything together in a neat little pouch. The entrepreneurial journey is about exploration, adventure and evolving. In order to grow and obtain our dreams at the highest levels, we have to step out of our comfort zones and explore the alternatives that are trying to get our attention.

These alternatives might not seem logical to us when they are presented, however, learning how to color outside the lines in life invites us to change the rules of engagement for how we show up with a new order or standard for service to humanity.

Conclusion
Changing the Rules

As I began creating a new business framework and changing the rules of engagement for how I was going to begin showing up in my entrepreneurship, I was so concerned about doing things the quote on quote right way towards taking the steps of embarking on the right paths to accomplish my goals.

A colleague of mine observed my behavior and suggested that I become like a house off of the grid to get a fresh perspective before moving forward. At first, I wasn't quite sure what she meant about the whole coming off the grid thing, yet once she explained that it would be a great assist in the re-ordering and re-alignment of my vision, I was totally open to allow the process to naturally unfold.

I surrendered my current view of my desires to allow higher levels of truth for my life and business to present itself. At first, it was a little challenging to imagine possibly not having my goal to materialize a certain way. Yet, there was comfort in knowing that if the universe had not opened up the opportunity for me to step more fully into my desires, then there was something greater and more aligned waiting to unfold.

I learned that the art of surrender at this point was not about totally giving up on what I wanted, but it was about allowing another way for success to present itself by providing a greater perspective for purpose and possibility.

If you've ever observed a house that is off of the grid, it is lifted off of the traditional foundation and often allows you see underneath the actual framework. This provides us with an opportunity to see what is really going on underneath the surface reality of our business.

Changing the rules and being off of the grid allows us to see how our life plan and business frameworks are now elevated. We look at our situation and see other alternatives. Instead of looking head on and only being able to see through a limited lens, not being so close to the situation invites us to become limitless in our view.

Great shifts occur when you become a house off the grid because every decision that you make is already being made from a higher perspective, raising the energy to co-create higher dreams for your life.

Though coming off the grid might feel like you have to give up at the moment that which you've been holding space for, the results for how it re-aligns your life-script is vibrationally and undeniably one of the best game changers for creating a lifestyle and business bigger than you've ever envisioned.

Conscious Business Game Changers Planning Section

Conscious Business Planning

Create an action plan for the week or month in the space below from the insights you've gained from the reading.

More Notes:

Becoming A Conscious Business Game Changer

Conscious Business Planning

Create an action plan for the week or month in the space below from the insights you've gained from the reading.

More Notes:

Becoming A Conscious Business Game Changer

Conscious Business Planning

Create an action plan for the week or month in the space below from the insights you've gained from the reading.

More Notes:

Becoming A Conscious Business Game Changer

Conscious Business Planning

Create an action plan for the week or month in the space below from the insights you've gained from the reading.

More Notes:

Becoming A Conscious Business Game Changer

Conscious Business Planning

Create an action plan for the week or month in the space below from the insights you've gained from the reading.

More Notes:

Becoming A Conscious Business Game Changer

Conscious Business Planning

Create an action plan for the week or month in the space below from the insights you've gained from the reading.

More Notes:

Becoming A Conscious Business Game Changer

Conscious Business Planning

Create an action plan for the week or month in the space below from the insights you've gained from the reading.

More Notes:

Becoming A Conscious Business Game Changer

Conscious Business Planning

Create an action plan for the week or month in the space below from the insights you've gained from the reading.

More Notes:

Becoming A Conscious Business Game Changer

Conscious Business Planning

Create an action plan for the week or month in the space below from the insights you've gained from the reading.

More Notes:

Becoming A Conscious Business Game Changer

Conscious Business Planning

Create an action plan for the week or month in the space below from the insights you've gained from the reading.

More Notes:

Becoming A Conscious Business Game Changer

Conscious Business Planning

Create an action plan for the week or month in the space below from the insights you've gained from the reading.

More Notes:

Becoming A Conscious Business Game Changer

Conscious Business Planning

Create an action plan for the week or month in the space below from the insights you've gained from the reading.

More Notes:

Becoming A Conscious Business Game Changer

Conscious Business Planning

Create an action plan for the week or month in the space below from the insights you've gained from the reading.

More Notes:

Conscious Business Planning

Create an action plan for the week or month in the space below from the insights you've gained from the reading.

More Notes:

Becoming A Conscious Business Game Changer

Record Highlights From Your Overall Conscious Business Planning Experience

Record Highlights From Your Overall Conscious Business Planning Experience

Becoming A Conscious Business Game Changer

Record Highlights from Your Overall Conscious Business Planning Experience

Record Highlights from Your Overall Conscious Business Planning Experience

For More Resources

www.consciouscorporatestrategies.blogspot.com

www.amazon.com/author/alicianwaters

Or

To Book the Author

For Speaking Engagements

Email: www.anwempires@gmail.com

If you enjoyed this resource, please consider writing a review on Amazon.com

Thanks & Blessings!

www.ingramcontent.com/pod-product-compliance
Lightning Source LLC
Chambersburg PA
CBHW071819170526
45167CB00003B/1373